The Conflict Resolution Library™

Dealing with Someone Who Won't Listen

• Lisa K. Adams •

The Rosen Publishing Group's
PowerKids Press™
New York

Published in 1997 by The Rosen Publishing Group, Inc.
29 East 21st Street, New York, NY 10010

First Edition

Book Design: Erin McKenna

Photo Credits: Cover by Thomas Mangieri; pp. 4, 7, 16 © S. Feld/H. Armstrong Roberts, Inc.; pp. 8, 19 © H. Armstrong Roberts, Inc.; p. 11 © Ron Chapple/FPG International Corp.; p. 12 © D. Logan/H. Armstrong Roberts, Inc.; p. 15 © Blumebild/H. Armstrong Roberts, Inc.; p. 20 © Lafoto/H. Armstrong Roberts, Inc.

Adams, Lisa K.
　　Dealing with someone who won't listen / by Lisa K. Adams.
　　　　p.　　cm. — (The conflict resolution library)
　　Includes index.
　　Summary: Discusses the nature of listening, the problem of dealing with someone
　　who will not listen, and what to do about it.
　　ISBN 0-8239-5074-3
　　1. Listening—Juvenile literature. [1. Listening.] I. Title. II. Series.
　　BF323.L5A33 1997
　　153.6'8—dc21
                                                                                   97-1297
                                                                                     CIP
                                                                                      AC

Manufactured in the United States of America

Contents

What Is Listening?

Listening is more than just hearing sounds. It takes **concentration** (kon-sen TRAY-shun) to be a good listener. You have to work hard to understand what you hear. When you are listening to somebody else, you have to think about what he or she is saying. Listening means learning to **appreciate** (uh-PREE-she-ayt) another person's thoughts and ideas.

When someone isn't listening to you, remember that listening can be hard to do. Maybe you can help that person learn to be a good listener.

◀ Good listeners often make good friends.

Why Don't People Listen?

There can be many reasons why someone doesn't listen to you. He may be busy and just can't listen at that moment. He may not be interested in what you have to say. Or he may not know how to listen to others.

Some people are bad listeners. Often you must try hard to get a person to listen to you.

It can hurt your feelings when someone doesn't listen to you. ▶

I'm Frustrated!

Have you ever tried to talk to your parents, and they don't seem to be listening? Have you ever told a story to a friend only to find out that she wasn't listening? That can make you feel **frustrated** (FRUS-tray-ted).

We have all been in situations where we are trying to talk to someone and they don't seem to be listening.

◀ Everyone has felt like no one is listening to them at one time in their lives.

Getting Angry

If you think that someone isn't listening to you, don't let your frustration make you angry. If you get angry and raise your voice, the person you are talking to may get angry too. The talk might turn into an **argument** (AR-gyoo-ment). Then no one will listen!

If you do get angry, let some time pass before you try to talk to the person again. That way you can both calm down. Then you will be able to talk about the problem and listen to each other.

If you think you might get angry at someone who isn't listening, give yourself a chance to calm down before ▶ trying to talk to that person again.

When Someone Won't Listen

If you want someone to listen, you must first get his or her **attention** (uh-TEN-shun). The best way to do this is by saying "excuse me" or "listen to this." Once you get the person's attention, speak calmly. This way, he or she will be more likely to listen to you.

Then it's your turn to listen. By talking and listening to each other, you can have a good **discussion** (dis-KUSH-un). If both people listen, both people will be heard.

◀ Having a good discussion means that both people are listening to each other.

When Parents Don't Listen

Sometimes it's hard to get your parents to listen to you. Parents are very busy people. They want to listen to you, but there are times when they may not be able to.

Be smart and pick a good time to talk to your parents. If your mom is on the phone, wait until she gets off the phone before you talk to her. That way, she can focus her full attention on you.

Parents have a lot to do. If they don't listen to you at a certain time, wait until they have a free ▶ moment before you try to talk to them again.

Jake Learns About Listening

Jake was building a model car, but he couldn't figure out which paint and stickers would look best. Jake needed some **advice** (ad-VYS). Jake found his dad, who was cooking dinner in the kitchen. Even though he wanted help right away, Jake saw that his dad was really busy. Jake asked his dad if they could talk about his car after dinner. His dad said, "Sure thing!"

After dinner, Jake's dad had plenty of time to talk with Jake about his car.

◀ You may have better luck getting someone to listen to you if you wait for a good time to talk.

Listening and Agreeing

When someone **disagrees** (DIS-uh-GREEZ) with you, you may feel that he or she is not listening.

Kara asked her parents if she could go to her friend Ryan's house and play with his new video game. Her parents told her that it wasn't a good day since Aunt Betsy was coming to visit. Kara could play with Ryan tomorrow.

Kara got angry. "You never listen to me!" she yelled. But her parents had listened.

Getting upset and yelling will not make someone listen to you. ▶

Being a Good Listener

Kara's parents had understood her when she said she wanted to play at Ryan's house. Having listened, they explained why that day wasn't a good day.

But all Kara heard was "no." She didn't listen to the rest of what her parents said. Instead, she got angry.

If Kara wants her parents to listen to her and respect her ideas, then she must do the same for them.

◄ When you listen to another person's ideas and opinions, she will listen to what you want to say too.

Your Voice Counts!

Everybody wants to be heard. It's frustrating when people don't listen to what you have to say. Every person's thoughts and ideas are important, including yours.

We all want to **express** (ex-PRES) ourselves. We have to work together to make sure everyone gets a chance to be heard.

Glossary

advice (ad-VYS) Giving an opinion about something.

appreciate (uh-PREE-she-ayt) To think highly of someone or something.

argument (AR-gyoo-ment) When people disagree.

attention (uh-TEN-shun) Carefully looking at or listening to something or someone.

concentration (kon-sen-TRAY-shun) Focusing your thoughts and attention on one thing.

disagree (DIS-uh-GREE) To believe or feel something different from what another person thinks.

discussion (dis-KUSH-un) A talk about something.

express (ex-PRES) To let others know what you feel and think.

frustrated (FRUS-tray-ted) When someone is bothered or annoyed.

Index